A MASQUE OF POETRY

by

Thomas Thornburg

ISBN: 978-1-60174-906-2

For Merle Fifield

DRAMATIS PERSONAE

THE POET

LUCIFERA, QUEEN OF NIGHT

LUCIFER, PRINCE OF DARKNESS

AURORA, GODDESS OF DAWN

DANCERS

[When the curtain opens, the time is evening in a deserted grove. The stage is bare. Music is heard. The Poet enters and in elaborate gesture and demeanor shows his fear and uncertainty at having found himself in such surroundings. He bears in his hand a manuscript; he wears at his waist an ink flask and a quill. He moves to stage center, where there is placed a riser surmounted by a stark thicket. After his opening sonnet, the Poet will lie down upon the riser; i.e., in the thicket.]

POET:

> He thieves at Poetry that hath in love,
> Confounding what cannot be copulate,
> Filched by bright Reason's rule in that estate
> Dark Passion's is, admitting none above;
> So am I fled to this sad grove
> Where love unlanguaged cannot advocate,
> Nor intellect convict dispassionate,
> Nor poem but prate, nor any passion prove.
> The lie of Passion is to promise proof
> To stolen evenings that there lives no day;　　10
> Self-serving rant the wrong of Reason's lies,
> As Love star-chambered, 'neath her sable roof
> Mourns her lost consort, powerless to say,
> The Poet reft of his quintessence dies.

[Poet sleeps. Dissolve to night. Dancers as stars appear. A ballet in largo is performed. At close of ballet the stars adore a descending crescent moon. Enter Lucifera. In her right hand she bears a black veil and a silvered mask of a young girl. In her left hand she bears a silver mask of death.]

LUCIFERA:

Now sound me the sennet, now ruffle me tuckets,
Ye stalkers of night in attendance nocturnal,
Crepuscular creatures who rove where stoats suck;
O'er stoned boors distill me now darkness diurnal,
Rare juices of summer, the ripe rusk of autumn,
Dank sepses secrete me that musk there the
    churning   20
Disturbance of day-cares I spurn in my vaunting
Denial of duteous toadies to dawn.
Rush high, now, now rush us such wild highs that
    haunt these
Quotidian tedious factotums and fawners.
Dull fact's purse of virtues can purchase no cunning
Where I, Lucifera, turn tricks all my own.
Dark gall'ries are hung now where boys tie my
    buntings,
As Paladins palely they ride in their dreams;
There perky girls jerkined will grin at my shunts;
In halls far removed from their cold kitchened
    seamstresses,   30
Hautboys and fellows of cello may lap me,

There honey-lipped Pindars will rape me in reams;
Where leather-legged visions by four fast joints strap
    me
(It pleases what teases them me cannot open),
Cold queries and sad habits praise my perhaps.
Behold! (Me beholden the dead eyes of dopers
Beholding bring gold boys to brighten my night);
Behold these sweet legions who live without hope.
Behold me. Though beholding beware of such
    sights:
For me was proud Pentheus led to his slaughter,   40
For me was Orion bereft of his light,
For me was rare Daphne struck dumb by clear
    waters,
For me was fleet Actaeon hounded to Hell,
For me wept Niobe bereft of her daughters,
For me poor Tarpeia sold all she could sell.
In me behold every dark unofficial
Remembrance of Time puling books cannot tell:
On the island of Knossos by signs sacrificial
The dancers symbolically writhe as they strow
The tarn and the turf by the ancient initial,   50
For me every sweet thing condemned beyond
    knowing
In flame reversed, gowned to the dull muffled
    drum,
Set upon, set afire (by whose members set glowing?)
Go lashed to the stakes there, erected and dumb.

Behold! Mad-cap Meg, pretty Peg strut their
   mumming
My tricks for all comers. Prithee, won't you come?

[Lucifera dances a largo with the stars. THE MOON
ASCENDS. EXIT DANCERS. After her dance,
Lucifera discovers Poet. She addresses Poet.]

LUCIFERA:
   One fine day when Winter find thee
   Secret in the wintered thicket,
   Where wind-whipped small sleet remind thee
   And the crow's malevolent cry   60
   Casting skyward into Winter
   O'er the stubbled glare that blind thee,
   Winter on thy eye.
   One fine day when Winter cheer thee
   Burbling into Spring around thee,
   Sexton-of-the-woods surround thee,
   Violet and Pansy eye,
   Sweet Anemone unground thee,
   And the dawn-bird's dawning cry
   Find thee deaf to fear.   70
   One fine day when Summer quicken
   Root and bole in summer glade
   (wherein once a winter thicket)
   Pan and parolee of Hades,

Nymph and Dryad, Lords and Ladies,
Wain and wight and girl and boy
(Quick! the summer bird, Quick, Quick!)
Only morning's sleepy cricket,
Only mourning dove,
After so much summer's turbulence   80
Disturb their joy,
Their love.
One fine day when wild Fall swing thee
In a kiting wind that bring thee
Home, Tithonous, to thy lover,
Black or blood or blonde bedraggle
Hill and drowsy dale where stagger
Summer's bacchic bagatelle,
Bleachéd runes of Time discover
Thee the Dream that is no other: 90
To the cracked Earth of the Mother
In a westering wind that chill thee
Death will top the hill to kill thee.
But for now
Nor rain nor snow
Tarantell nor tempest shake thee
Not until
My burning will
To know thee and my hunger fill
For this I turn and turning,   100
Wake thee.

[Lucifera wakes Poet at this point. Poet sits up and beholds her in wonder. Lucifera royally gestures Poet to rise, which he does.]

LUCIFERA:

> What child is this so late upon my lawn,
> So velvet-chested and so legged in fawn,
> So sound a sleeper? How so are you come
> To these wild regions wandered; where your home?
> Are you some student wearied of his book,
> In fortune failing whom his friends forsook?
> So might you be, to my unpracticed eye,
> Orion's image fallen from the sky.
> Are you that swimmer, swum into my ken,   *110*
> Re-born a youth into this world of men?
> But inky finger and a spill of ink
> By this small button where these gussets sink
> Would seem a student still, but stiller how?
> Yet here's some further matter we needs know:
> What are these characters upon this sheet?
> Are students rhymers now, and do ye greet
> Your masters (mentors call ye?) all in rhymes,
> And thus rolls taken at your meeting times?
> Did *teum*, *meum*, mark that budding frown   *120*
> Set on your cheek? Do women now go gowned?
> La, how I chatter! be these scholar's hands?
> Still, I perceive no signet here; no bands

Proclaim thee bedded. . . *wedded* to thy book,
But still. . . how came you by that pensive look?
Is this a quill whose rigid nib so fine
Is herein trammeled where your closures line?
Bring me my tablets! would you me indict
Some token on a virgin sheet this night?
My jesting does not take you; still, 'twere best   *130*
If all things taken taken were in jest,
And so when all are lessoned, which is more?
Say, are you scholar? School me, I implore.

POET:

Lady, how I hither came
Where a vagrant sleep o'ercame me,
Hither came or whither go
In a dream that me so seizes,
Now my presence thee displeases
And occasions me some grief,
I do not know.   *140*

LUCIFERA:

You do not know.

POET:

I do not know. What dreads of night
Await me here? I hither came
When every else had failed of solace

Nor any single sconce to light me
Directionless and without blame,
Nor do I know this place.

LUCIFERA:

Dear boy, you do not know.

POET:

I neither know, nor never knowing
Beauty, grandeur such as yours,   *150*
Nor no such touch as sets me glowing,
Nor never thought to know, nor thought
To wake to such a potent hour:
Was this in seeking what I sought?
I did not, do not, know.

LUCIFERA:

No?

POET:

Yes.

LUCIFERA:

Yes — ?

POET:

I do not know if no be yes.
Except you see me so accouter'd   160
No, am not drunk, no scholar I;
Though these be letters, am unlettered,
My words all failed of charm. Here fettered,
Feckless here, and reft of song,
My times are steeped so much in wrong,
I cannot write.

LUCIFERA:

Wrong to right?

POET:

O, even wrong to write!

LUCIFERA:

Dear boy, young sir, how serendipitous
That seeking Truth as every Poet ought   170
You fetch upon these altars and are thus

POET:

Discovered

LUCIFERA:

And discover all you sought

POET:

Lady, wherefore. . . .

LUCIFERA:

Where the droning bee doth daily browse
Among his herded lilies, and the rose
Doth yield her fragrance to his nappy clothes,
Bescented courier of summer's vows,
Above the barley and the rye

POET:

Sweet scenes of summer!   *180*

LUCIFERA:

Like that hummer,
In thy mind's eye, fly.
Or on languorous evenings such as these
Where madly banking twitter-bats carom
About the eave's drop, lovers take their ease

POET:

And live life eas'ly

LUCIFERA:

Word it as you please,
But at that velvet hour when death doth come,

The dead do rise, and day doth his obeisance
Pay there, fix that in thy dance.   *190*
And when the querulous robin, quarreling jay
Or mourning dove doth all the morning moan
His lot upon the willow, where the sun
Hath through its branch venetianed so the pond
(Where swim the speckled trout in prism'd day)
Doth seem a wond'rous world to whom belong

POET:

Such faery creatures!

LUCIFERA:

Such as live within thy song.
Such is that other world, they say, who seem
To live within it, they that word it: Dream.   *200*

[Poet falters and lies back down on riser. Lucifera places mask of death on Poet, and veil of night. Lucifera now calls forth DANCERS FROM STAGE RIGHT AND LEFT, which dancers appear in very sinister poses, clad in leaves and flowers. They should be making the signs of horns on their heads, suggestive of the whole spirit of the dance and also suggestive of cuckoldry.]

LUCIFERA:

Haste thee, nymphs, and bring with thee

Trophies of the chase and flee,
Stag-horns top thy tousled heads
Proof of lust and loosened beds,
Thracian women, dance my round,
'Til Eurydice go down
Down again into that Hell
All who love know: Kiss and Tell

DANCERS CHORUS:

Kiss and Tell
Kiss and Tell   210
All who love know: Kiss and tell

LUCIFERA:

Was it Orpheus so loved,
So uxorious he moved
Heaven first, who then moved Hades
(Wherein dwell fine lords and ladies)
That their king delivered up
At that hour when hunters sup
(I.e., when their pleasure's done)
A living woman Death had won.
Yet, upon their going up   220
At that hour when hunters sup
Something glistered in the eye
Of this *wife* Eurydice
Caused our Orpheus to look
And at that instant she was struck

Dead again, and dead returned
To that King for whom she. . . *burned.*
This strange story I relate
In the interests of that state
Of being: all things copulate.   230
Hear me now and mark me well
All who love know: Kiss and Tell

CHORUS:

Kiss and Tell
Kiss and Tell
All who love know: Kiss and Tell

LUCIFERA:

Is it not a faery thing?
That of whom the muses sing?
Did the thought of leaving her
Cause his thoughtless glance unsure?
Or did something else he saw   240
Still his lilting music? Or
Did he see within the eye
Of this *wife* Eurydice
Mirrored there as water turned
Visage of the King for whom she... *burned?*
Some relate this Orpheus bled
For the wife whom he left dead.
Others say that maids in Thrace
Tore his loins from out their place.

But who can tell us what he saw   250
Halting in the yawning maw
Of Hell itself when first he gazed
On a woman Hell had razed,
And in seeing that saw Hell:
All who love know: Kiss and Tell

CHORUS:

Kiss and Tell
Kiss and Tell
All who love know: Kiss and Tell

[Dancers dance together in andante. Then DANCERS
EXIT right and left.]

LUCIFERA:

Often in the evening
At the dying day   260
You may hear my mongers,
Hear them at their play,
You may hear them piping
Merrily away,
Merrily as children, hear them as they say:
RIPE, CHERRY, RIPE CHERRY, CHERRY,
     CHERRY, RIPE
Taste the golden apples, or a pungent plum

Mouth our Mandarin oranges; from the East they
   come,

Oranges of Joppa, succulent the fig;

Berries will we bring you, bright and blush and
   big;   270

Eat them and discover innocence again,

Pregnant with their powers, surcease from your
   pain;

Fuzzy, muzzy peaches, succulent delights;

All my mongers carry licenses to marry:

RIPE, CHERRY, RIPE CHERRY, CHERRY,
   CHERRY RIPE

Hear them in the evening where the sleepy bird

Echoes in the dove-cote every lilting word

Aubades for my coming, tendering the Night:

RIPE, CHERRY, RIPE CHERRY, CHERRY,
   CHERRY RIPE

[ENTER FAUNS, SATYRS, AND LES HOMMES
SAUVAGES. They dance a hornpipe. After the
hornpipe they try to capture the NYMPHS in vivace.
Now dancers begin to circle Poet, grotesquely dancing
the dance of the bear as Lucifera instructs them to
torture the Poet in all his dreams.)

LUCIFERA:

Bear him, now bear him, now bear him such
   dreams   280

Poems are pulséd by; dance him such scenes

Move him to marvels beyond human caring,
Dance him, my children, the Dance of the Bear.
Safe in his thicket the Bear lies a-dreaming,
Dreaming of Summer, the full summer bough,
The fish in his fjord, the mountain cat keening
Her lost velvet lover, where wild wolves are prowling
Free as the moonlight, the masked badger scowling
Runs away, runs away, where maenads are howling
Wild by the river the rat keeps his lair   290
As we dance him, my children, the Dance of the
     Bear.
Once where I danced in the circus of Troy
Bosséd and greaved in a carnage of shambles
Wildly in love there each red bleeding boy
Capered and cut there in blood to the ankle,
Achilles, Patroc'lus and Hector in joy fell,
Wildly in love there they met death uncaring,
Dancing there, prancing the Dance of the Bear.
Milk-white entranced there and far from the battle
Helen lay drugged to her dugs in a tub,   300
Smiling the day through as maids in their prattle
Anointed her shoulders in cascades of bubbles,
And all through the Night when Andromache
     weeping
Mourned her doomed love of the bright shining
     hair,
Helen and Paris lay twined in their sleep
Dreaming the dream of the Dance of the Bear.
Wildly, my children, I spun in the slaying,

Dabbled my hands in the red of the slain,
Musking the wine of my pride until day-fall,
Old Priam perceiving perceived his life painful,   310
And the bitch-goddess Hera perceiving me there
Lictored me soundly for Dancing the Bear.
Therefore to this night in the wild dance of Time
We whirl in the darkness, immortal, uncaring,
To every such sort as are up-attic rhyming
Their bright books entrancing: The Dance of the
    Bear:
Dance him now, dance him the Dance of the Bear.

[Dancers circle Poet in dance, then EXIT right and
left. THE CRESCENT MOON DESCENDS FROM
ALOFT.]

LUCIFERA:

Mark now how my lover to me cometh,
Mark now how his rising in the Night
Sure as the astrolabe doth to me hometh   320
And he me doth encompass in his light;
Thus are we met at each meridian line
And nightly as the gloaming owl complains
Are we made one, so fixéd and co-joined
And, wakeful to our dawns, go joined again.
Mark now, or any several moonrise, mark
His self ascending to my crescent form,

The darkened world in us made double-dark
As love untroubled sweetly lies until the morn.
Thus is the Night bedizened but forlorn,   *330*
The stars themselves being of our blisses born,
And every lyric of our faded losses made
Doth fill the night with music, and doth fade.
On such a night as this did Heaven's Hound
Unleashed upon bold Lucifer secure
This lawless round, and thus, the sages say,
God fixed delight's own door where men endure,
Imprisoned there, the sterile light of day.
O, demon lover, hovering o'er my hill,
Be-shroud me in thy darkened light, eclipse,   *340*
Be-still my searéd soul, and seal my lips,
And bid the busied birds of day be still.

[Enter Lucifer. In his right hand he cradles the lamp of darkness. He is a striking figure, but of course quite sinister, and his speech will show his futile and exacerbating anger at Art, the Poet as artist, and any idea of Art as providing illumination for men's souls. He grandly returns Lucifera's greeting, which she royally extends him with her *left* hand (each saluting the other from the sinister side), aloft and arrested. Then Lucifera gestures evilly towards the Poet, whom Lucifer approaches and addresses thus:]

LUCIFER:

Here is a dream for you.

[Poet tosses in his sleep.]

Erichthos,
Homunculus,
Anaxagoras,
Thales,
This one works if another such fails,
One hates Poets as I hate jails,
One is in a bottle, one is in a dream,   350
The pet-cocks pop where another one steams,
One rants reason while another one rails,
Chop their tops and drop 'em into pails:
Erichthos,
Homunculus,
Anaxagoras,
Thales.
Or would you prefer another dream?
Quick-Loot and Grabber sitting in a ditch
Glimming all the nereids the pitch-forks pitch,   360
Helen has, Paris has — how I itch!
Counting-out lies about who got what,
Tommy-rot, tommy-rot, tommy-rot, rot!
In came Galatea, riding in a shell
Whoops! and away again, riding pell-mell,
Make haste! not a taste! nay, nor e'en a smell!
Ha, ha! Proteus thinks he is in Hell
Do tell!
Listen to my children, watch how they bleed:

Want   *370*
Debt
Care
Need.

[Poet tosses feverishly here in his dream]

    Or perhaps you would like *another* dream:
    Erichthos, Erichthos, here's your bait;
    Tickle his fancy and make it wait,
    Stout-car, double-jar, carry my freight,
    Play him a suit we all can Hate!

[Here Lucifer poses and postures, ironically showing
the stupidity of all clothes horses. . . *a la* Richard III's
Looking Glass speech.]

    Behold my celery hat!
    Behold my vest of puppy-skin!   *380*
    Behold my cape of lemon-cake
    Behold my shoes of guppies!
    A kitten for my collar,
    A shirt of prancing kirsch,
    A three-piece suit of banyan-root
    Or wear the vest reversed.
    I eat a bowl of guano
    I drink a cup of jute!
    Or standing tall, I take it all

And stuff it in my smoot!   *390*
Gobble! Gobble! Gobble!

[Demonic laughter]

Enough. . . enough. . . enough.

[Now Lucifer advances downstage and addresses audience, speaking the following:]

LUCIFER:

Should the night and the mists of the moon
   miscarry,
And the heathy thicket of summer's spell
Sadly fade in the dell of the land of faery,
What children would listen to songs you tell?
At the back of the wind are the dark cars flashing,
Their wheels flash fire 'til the dawn of day,
And they race away into Time be-dashing
Bright coins spent along the way.   *400*
Mark how the bird of night doth warble
His monody sad, until dawn o'clock
Awakens the world to its day of trouble,
And the raucous shrilling of brazen cocks.
Approacheth the hour of the busied trundle,
Of carking noons and the groaning freight
Of the round world's lading by box and bundle

In the workaday world of man's estate.
Only the night hath him provided
Nostrum nocturnal where she may kiss   410
At his own leisure, and, un-derided,
He lie with her there and not be missed.
Thus are his songs entire compriséd
Of loves remembered, or of her not yet,
And thus is the night itself deviséd
That, having suffered, they may forget.

[Dawn begins to break. Lucifer perceives it. He moves to Lucifera.]

O, damnéd, damnéd light!
We must away.
Lead thou our darkness into damnéd day.

[Lucifer and Lucifera dance a stately galliard, Lucifer holding aloft the lamp of darkness. A bell sounds. LUCIFER and LUCIFERA EXIT. MOON ASCENDS. Dissolve into golden day. Dancers enter, clad as sunbeams. SUN DESCENDS. Sunbeams adore the sun. Aurora ENTERS. Aurora's opening aubade:]

AURORA:

I mark the birds beginning   420
To tell the tale of Dawn,
Where all the darkness waning

Strews summer on the lawn;
Could love endure forever
Wonder might never wane,
But still chill seasons sever
Where lovers languish, paired in pain.
O, mark the birded morning
And truss it to your hearts,
That every season borning   430
May summer still, when winters part you;
Therefore, in stillest dawnings
I home you with a word:
What though it all, my loves, were past recall?
The dawn's a singing bird.

[Slash indicates breath pause.]

Great god for whom the seasons in their splendours
    do diurnal roll /
About this measured round upon which man doth
    know his mortal sphere
Of days, / and doth by trope and ploy figúrative
    attempt the fixéd measure of his questing soul, /
A time to plant and thence to reap, and mark
    himself there measured, hear, O, hear /
O, thou for whom the blushéd buds of roses in
    their arbored ways do turn   440
Their crimson cheeks / as there they bathe within
    the light cascading from thy urns /

O, thou for whom the verdant corn doth lift her
    yellow tassels to the nodding noon /

Wherein in fixéd rows the plowman and his
    consort dally in their golden summer's swoon /

O, thou for whom the mighty steeds of day in
    skying daring do bestride /

The singletree of thy meridian line whereon in thy
    fixed courses in the brazen car you ride /

Thy fixéd solstices which halve and quarter all the
    spanning years /

That man may know and, gladsome in the whirling
    hub of day unending, praise thee /

Hear, O hear.

Man-killer, man-preserver,

Far-darter, bright destroyer, thou who heard /   *450*

And having granted Phaeton his boon to go
    bewingéd as a bird, /

And heard the prayer of Demeter who burned in
    drought, /

Thou struck the sounding chimes of judgment's
    scale and cast him out; /

Thus thy stern justice o'er the sterile world held
    sway, /

Even as thy own beloved son fell flaming into day. /

[She cries out to the god:]

Apollo, Apollo, Apollo! /
Cast now thy golden beams of day, into men's sight
Cascading, / and cast back the night!

[The sunbeams dance in adoration and discover the Poet. They lift the veil of night and run in terror from the mask of death. Aurora approaches the Poet.]

AURORA:

Here lies within the veil of night
A sorry thing, a sorry need,   460

[She removes the veil of night from the Poet.]

And with the mask of Death bedight
A sorry need, a sorry thing.

[She removes the mask of Death]

Upon his countenance alight
And with thy beams do thou embright
This Poet, this wond'rous voice who sings
The word-hoard of all naméd things.
Awake! Awake! Awake!

[She wakes Poet and gestures that he rise, which he does. *This is a stern, no-nonsense question:*]

How camest thou here?

POET:

[Stammering confusedly, he tries to recount his experience]

What dreams! What visions here impress me!
What dews are these, what airs here dress me?   *470*
What fiendish, foolish thoughts possess?
What beasts were those? What nosing cat
Beclad in crepe and silent paw
Supped at my heart?
A celery hat!
A Chorus there of jacks and daws!
Vast hornéd things, a splendid hell
Comprised of darkness visible!
And double-dark within my mind
They yet reside, and do resound   *480*
Upon my deafened ear, and blinded
Here I fell into a damnéd swound!
I am dashed into fragments, and must tell
Through fearful art the awful truths of Hell!

AURORA:

Be silent in the golden light of day.

[This is a stern, direct command. She is telling the Poet to shut up and hear the truth.]

The reason why men sit to write is this:
They sadly quest to call up all the dead,
And yet, become enamoured, they do kiss
Their learnéd book and Life do find instead.
 Thus in the human merriment of Art   *490*
They find their quittance from that sadder part
That once them summoned.
When he must suffer, his dark hour come,
In that dark midnight of the Poet's soul,
Do thou remember, and this truth extol:
He hymns the death of all the dying dumb.
Woman and man, bright girl and vagrant boy
On death's high way to chant his song of joy
Sauntéring there, they go their holy ways
In Life's bright failure he must, praising, praise. *500*
This is that death that Daedelus, discerning,
Bright artificer, on his own begotten clay,
He fixed the wingéd art that rose him burning,
And him cast headlong into burning day.
Thus is that death old Aegeus, perceiving
The careless shroud of his funéreal sail,
Thought Theseus dead and all his questing failed,
Dove headlong down into the sea of grief.
Thus is the death each man must die, but, harken:
Some in their questing mile-stones do impart   *510*
To every several harker's homing, marking
The joyous vistas of their human art.
This is the glad bright hymnal of the human heart.

How but in joy hath every human sorrow
Been there preservéd, and in joy endured,
How but in joy hath every bright tomorrow
Been therein promised, word on careful word?
How but in joy?

[Poet kneels before Aurora, who places the laurel on Poet's head.]

Poet, by this sign be blessed:
Homo faber ludens est.   520
And in thy fearful human quest
Bear this badge upon thy breast:
Homo ludens,
Homo loquens summum bonum est.

[Aurora extends hands in blessing upon Poet as SUN ASCENDS. Poet, now stage center, delivers closing sonnet to audience:]

POET:

Mark now how every starréd night doth fade
Into dissolvéd else at every dawn,
As any several star-lit promise made
Must stand arrested in the circuit sun.
Did not on such an evening God's first man
Begin to set the sealéd name of things   530

Until her love bewitched him so, he ran
And drank the fruit that every Poet sings?
In darksome day distilling they perceived
The poignant song of every poem sung:
As celebrants they sang their father's grief,
And joy went worded in their mother tongue.
Accept, great Queen, our hymn of joy to thee
In this thy year of silver jubilee.

[CURTAIN]

A MASQUE OF POETRY – NOTES

This masque, composed and first produced in 1977, presents a popular Renaissance theme whose popularity in art, and whose usefulness as a philosophical paradigm, have endured to this day: the conflict between things Dionysian and Apollonian. In the present instance, I adopt Lucifera, Queen of Night, and inform her with the mythic properties commonly or uncommonly associated with Artemis in all her myriad roles. Her consort, Lucifer, is I think appropriately Faustian; the most of his lyrics are derived from various celebrations of Walpurgisnacht, principally that found in Goethe. Aurora of course I associate with Apollo. In no instance have I introduced any aspect of myth not found in standard texts of mythology, unless in the instance in which I permit Lucifera to advance a "new" idea regarding Orpheus' death (in the "Kiss and Tell" Chorus).

The lyrics for this masque are in the main composed in strict traditional forms, which any student of Poetry or any other craftsman may peruse at his leisure. Aurora's lyrics comprise the only potential difficulty for the prosodist; they are written in stress count. The vocabulary I have attempted in the masque ranges from standard school Latin (Aurora) to American slang of the sixties and seventies in Lucifera's first speech. The student of mythology may consult the following works to which I am indebted: Gayley's *Classic Myths*, Graves' *Mythology*, H. J. Rose's *Handbook of Greek Mythology*, the Aldington and Amers translation of *Larousse Mythologie Generale*, and Bullfinch's *Mythology*. The stagecraft for this masque is that employed by the greatest masquer, Inigo Jones, whose work may be surveyed in any standard history of the masque.

Of the many difficulties attendant upon presenting a masque in the first quarter of the twenty-first century, the greatest is to my mind that of convincing the players, schooled as they are in four centuries of theatre after the demise of the popular masque, that the masque is *allegorical* and *symbolic* in its intent rather than *histrionic* in the original sense of that term. In saying of *Comus* that

> Milton... is without dramatic sense
> or the sense of the stage, and the
> masque is full of monologues and
> lengthy tirades....

Emile Legouis and Louis Cazamian err in their appreciation for masque technique. Thus they say in their analysis of *Comus*, "Everything which might be dramatic is frozen or suppressed. The characters remain abstract as virtues or vices." Such criticism is much nearer the mark when it confesses that

> There are many charming, delicate
> descriptions in the masque, too subtle
> to be appreciated or even, perhaps,
> immediately understood, as they are
> heard on stage.

But in their final analysis, their egalitarianism thwarts their aesthetic appreciation for *Comus* as masque:

> The moral of the masque is Milton's moral — high, disdainful and solitary. The final impression is one of virtue remote from mankind and above it, sure and haughty virtue, ignoring the multitude. For the Milton of *Comus*, as for the Calvinists, the number of the elect is few. The Attendant Spirit guards, on his own showing, not the wicked or the half-good, but only the pure. These are chilly attitudes. How many who saw the masque played must have felt that they were excluded from the small band of the elect!

This argument is wrong because wrong-headed. Of the masque generally it is better to remark the caveat found in Baugh, *et al.*:

> The modern reader, who has before him only the prose synopses of the action and dry descriptions of the scenes and costumes and movement to supplement the texts, must reconstruct in his imagination the gorgeousness of these occasions.

No writer of a masque, short of seeing his work performed, could ask more.

Notes to the Lyrics

For the Poet's opening speech, a Petrarchan sonnet, I have in mind the workings of the historical Star Chamber for the topical allusion.

For Lucifera's opening address, I chose bacchic tetrameters in *terza rima*; the concept of "stoned" boors, "rushes," wild "highs," "tricks" turned, boys "tying off," and "shunts" is germane to American street argot of the 1960s and before; a heroin addict is said to tie-off his upper arm before injecting his drug; a whore is said to "turn tricks," one of her pelvic movements is known as a "shunt," etc. Artemis' association with Pentheus, Orion, Daphne, Actaeon, Niobe, and Ariadne (the island of Knossos) may be traced in any standard mythology; the sorry story of Tarpeia (hence, the "Rock Tarpeia" in *Horatius*) I recall from Plutarch's "Romulus."

In Lucifera's second speech, it is the common robin who is known as the Sexton of the Wood, which I recalled from an anonymous author of the seventeenth century, "How Robert the Robin spoke to the Eagle":

> ...for if I find a dead body in the
> wood, I and the rest of my fellows
> do bury it with moss and leaves, and
> for this I am called the Sexton of
> the Wood. (*The Pleasant History of
> Cawwood the Rooke....* 1640)

I have perhaps abused Poetic license in introducing the "tarantella" in this speech, but perhaps not when we recall that in one version of the myth of Orion and Artemis, the goddess caused a deadly scorpion to

sting Orion on the heel, thus causing his death and
exhibiting what the *Larousse Mythologie* calls "the dark
and vindictive character of Artemis."

Following Lucifera's colloquy with the Poet
(for which I chose echo-Poetry in part), I chose
trochaic tetrameter couplets (the "Kiss and Tell"
Chorus). Only in this instance have I departed from
received myth in permitting Lucifera's advancing a
"new" theory regarding Orpheus' death.

For Lucifera's *nocturne* (the "Ripe Cherry"
speech) I have in mind Rosetti's "Goblin Market."

For Lucifera's next speech (the "Dance of
the Bear") I chose dactylic tetrameters, masculine,
feminine, and occasional near rhymes. That the
Greeks were familiars to drugs *The Odyssey* makes
plain; Helen herself gives drugs to Telemachos in her
husband's palace. The "Dance of the Bear" and the
bear's thicket (the riser upon which the Poet reclines)
may be found most readily in *Larousse*, which calls a
statue of Artemis the *Artemis Brauronis*.

For the peroration of Aurora's speech, I sought
simply an amalgam of man working (*homo faber*),
man playing (*homo ludens*), and man languaged in his
highest form of art — Poetry (*homo loquens summum
bonum est*).

The Poet's closing Elizabethan sonnet ends
with the masque's dedication to Her Majesty Queen
Elizabeth II on the occasion of her silver jubilee.

Note on Music

Traditionally, a masque may involve instrumental music, dancing, and singing, at the producer's discretion. A *Masque of Poetry*, in its first production in 1977, included no singing, but a short overture and instrumental music accompanying the dances were composed for the occasion.

www.ingramcontent.com/pod-product-compliance
Lightning Source LLC
Chambersburg PA
CBHW060042040426
42331CB00032B/2239